My
Sense of Self

For Lou —
Hope you enjoy
sharing these
their life
Oct 10, 1988.

Donald Pelton

PUBLISHED BY
HELDON PRESS
9146 ARRINGTON AVE.
DOWNEY, CA. 90240

FIRST PRINTING JUNE 1984
SECOND PRINTING AUGUST 1985
ISBN 0-933169-01-9

FOR

RON

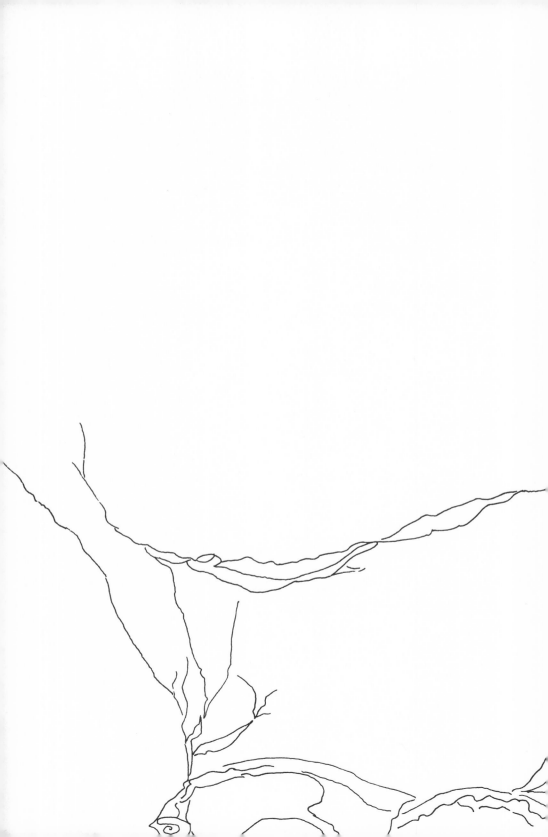

THIS ABOVE ALL
TO THINE OWN SELF ––

BE TRUE

SHAKESPEARE

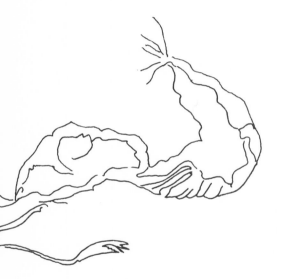

ACKNOWLEDGING THE CONTRADICTIONS
BETWEEN
WORD AND DEED

HOWEVER MANY HOLY WORDS YOU READ,

   HOWEVER MANY YOU SPEAK,

      WHAT GOOD WILL THEY DO YOU,

IF YOU DO NOT ACT UPON THEM?

        THE DHAMMAPADA

Prologue

MOST OF US CAN RECALL MOMENTS
WHEN WE HAVE REFLECTED UPON
ESPECIALLY MEANINGFUL INSIGHTS.
SOME OF US HAVE BEEN INCLINED
TO COMMUNICATE THESE THOUGHTS
VERBALLY. OTHERS OF US HAVE
PREFERRED TO SUBJECTIVELY
CONTEMPLATE OUR THOUGHTS,
KEEPING THEM TO OURSELVES.
SOME OF US HAVE A NEED TO
"WRITE IT DOWN".

THESE ARE NOTES, PERSONAL
REFLECTIONS, INSIGHTS, IN-
TUITIONS KNOWN THROUGH
EXPERIENCE ALONG THE WAY:
THOUGHTS TO BE SHARED —

A FEW-AFTERTHOUGHTS TO
ACADEMIC EXPERIENCES —

MANY-WHILE CONTEMPLATIVELY WALK-
ING-ALONG THE SEASHORE (CARMEL,
LAGUNA, LA JOLLA) MOST, HOWEVER,
DERIVED FROM REFLECTIVE, MEDITATIVE
"EXCURSIONS" LATE AT NIGHT.

ALL OF THEM-ATTEMPTS TO DISTILL
THE ESSENCE, FLESH OUT THE
MEANING, OF LIFE.

I HAVE NOT FOLLOWED A PRESCRIBED
OUTLINE OR STRUCTURE. RATHER,
I HAVE EXCERPTED, FROM THESE
PERSONAL JOURNALS, WHAT I
CONSIDER TO BE SIGNIFICANT
INSIGHTS ALONG THE WAY.

ANECDOTAL AND CASE HISTORY
REFERENCES, AS WITH FOOTNOTES
AND BIBLIOGRAPHY, HAVE BEEN
OMITTED BY DESIGN.

Contents

WITHOUT LEAVING HIS HOUSE,
ONE CAN KNOW EVERYTHING
THAT IS NECESSARY.

WITHOUT LEAVING HIMSELF,
ONE CAN GRASP ALL WISDOM.

LAO TZU

WE ARE MUCH WISER
THAN WE HAVE BEEN
LED TO BELIEVE.

Introduction

THESE ARE NOT NEW THOUGHTS.
YOU KNOW THEM.
THEY BELONG TO, ARE THE
HERITAGE OF
HUMANKIND.

CONFIRM FOR YOURSELF
THE TRUTH THAT LIES
WITHIN YOUR SELF

THE THOUGHTS BEING SHARED
ARE MEANT TO BE MULLED OVER,
THOUGHT ABOUT :
EXPERIENCED.
THE CONCEPTS SPEAK FOR
THEMSELVES.

FOR THOSE IN THE KNOW —
A REMINDER —
OF THINGS WE HAVE LEARNED —
AND MAY HAVE FORGOTTEN —

ALONG THE WAY.
FOR THOSE WHO WOULD LIKE TO KNOW—
AN INVITATION —
WE, AMONG ALL CREATURES,
HAVE BEEN ENDOWED WITH THE ABILITY
TO PERCEIVE — — — — — —A SENSE OF SELF.
WHEN WE EXPERIENCE A SENSE OF SELF
WE FEEL GOOD — ABOUT OURSELVES:
CONFIDENT, SECURE — FREE OF
INTIMIDATION — — — — FROM SELF OR OTHER.
— — — —FEEL GOOD ABOUT WHAT WE ARE
DOING — EXPERIENCE A SENSE OF
ACCOMPLISHMENT —
ARE NOT STRIVING — — — —
TO BE SOMEONE ELSE

WE ARE ALL ON A JOURNEY.
A PATH, SOME NOT SO AWARE OF THE
PATH AS OTHERS — VAGUELY AWARE——
OF HOW IT STARTED — MYSTIFIED AS TO
WHERE IT WILL END.

NO TWO PATHS WILL BE THE SAME,
EACH A UNIQUE REFLECTION OF
OUR INTUITION, OUR INNER-SELF.———

—ALL GOING IN THE SAME DIRECTION.

A SENSE OF SELF EVOLVES FROM
OUR CHOOSING THE RIGHT PATH---
THE ONE THAT BECKONS, FEELS
RIGHT : "FITS"

THE QUALITY OF OUR LIFE,
THE EXTENT TO WHICH IT IS
MEANINGFUL, HAS PURPOSE,
IS IN RELATION TO
THE PATH CHOSEN.

FOR AS LONG AS WE BREATHE ......
EACH MOMENT IS AN OPPORTUNITY
TO DISCOVER MEANING,
TO EXPERIENCE A PURPOSE
IN OUR LIVES,
TO NURTURE THE PROSPECT
OF REALIZING ....
PEACE OF MIND.

Mind

THE HUMAN MIND—
CLEANSED, PURGED OF
CONDITIONED PERCEPTIONS:
A SOURCE OF MIRACLES.

MIND SHOULD BE FREE TO GROW—
UNFETTERED, UNCONDITIONED —

CREATIVE, SEARCHING
TRANSCENDING THE MILIEU,
TRANSFORMING SELF.

THE HUMAN MIND, CLEANSED,
PURGED OF CONDITIONED PERCEPTIONS:
A SOURCE OF MIRACLES.

THEN, ONE DAY, I CHANGED
MY MIND AND
CHANGED MY WORLD.

TO BE AWARE OF THE
POTENTIAL — OF THE
HUMAN MIND (BIOCOMPUTER)
AND TO FAIL TO PROPERLY
PROGRAM (IT) —
IS TO FORFEIT OUR HUMANNESS

MIND CAN PRODUCE ANGUISH
OR DELIGHT.
WE PROGRAM FEAR —
WE CAN PROGRAM ECSTASY.

THE PURSUIT OF KNOWLEDGE
AS AN END IN ITSELF
IS A WASTE OF
OUR LIFE.

THE ESSENCE OF WISDOM
LIES IN ITS SUCCESSFUL
APPLICATION TO OUR DAILY
LIVES... DAY TO DAY, MOMENT
TO MOMENT
ESTABLISHING A CONGRUENCE
BETWEEN THOUGHT, WORD AND DEED

THE BODY IS A SUPPORT SYSTEM
FOR THE MIND
THE MIND: A SUPPORT SYSTEM
TO SPIRIT

HOW FRAGILE
THE MIND
HOW INCREDIBLE
ITS CAPACITY FOR ADAPTATION

Now

HOPE DOES NOT LIE IN AN
ILLUSORY FUTURE.

IT IS TO BE FOUND EXPERIENCING
THE PRESENT MOMENT
TO THE FULLEST.

YESTERDAY IS
ALREADY A DREAM
AND TOMORROW
IS ONLY A VISION:
BUT TODAY,
WELL LIVED,
MAKES EVERY
YESTERDAY
A DREAM OF
HAPPINESS AND
EVERY TOMORROW
A VISION OF
HOPE

FROM THE SANSKRIT

THE IDEAL SPECIAL PLACE WE SEEK IS
OURSELVES: WHERE WE HAPPEN TO BE--
CENTERED, AT PEACE WITH OURSELVES
EXPERIENCING THE GRACE OF THE MOMENT.

ATTEMPTS TO EXPLAIN THE PAST ARE
USUALLY DISTORTED AND SELF-SERVING.

HOPE DOES NOT LIE IN AN ILLUSORY FUTURE.
IT IS TO BE FOUND EXPERIENCING THE
PRESENT MOMENT TO THE FULLEST.

THERE IS ONLY THE PRESENT MOMENT.
TIME TAKEN FROM THE PRESENT
TO DWELL IN THE PAST
OR FANTASIZE ABOUT THE FUTURE,
BOTH OF WHICH ARE ILLUSION,
IS IRRETRIEVABLE.

FOCUSING OUR ATTENTION ON WHAT IS,
AS CONTRASTED TO WHAT OUGHT TO BE:

IS AS LIVING IS TO DYING.

EACH MOMENT OF OUR LIVES
IS AN OPPORTUNITY
TO DETACH OURSELVES
FROM THOSE ASPECTS
OF THE MILIEU
THAT ARE SELF-DEMEANING,
THAT INHIBIT THE EXPERIENCING
OF TRUE SELF:
FREEING OURSELVES
OF TRIVIA, ROUTINES,
STEREOTYPED BEHAVIOR.

WE CANNOT BE EVALUATING, LIKING OR
DISLIKING, WORRYING, REACTING, AND.....
EXPERIENCING THE BEAUTY OF THE MOMENT.

MIND CANNOT BE TWO PLACES AT THE SAME TIME.

IN THIS MOMENT THERE IS THE POSSIBILITY,
THE POTENTIAL, FOR CUTTING TIES WITH
ALL PREVIOUS MOMENTS · · · · · · · · · · · · · · · ·
TO FREE OURSELVES OF FEAR, GUILT,
INTIMIDATION.

NO ONE CAN TAKE THIS
            MOMENT FROM US
BUT OURSELVES.

RESISTANCE TO WHAT IS
            OF THE MOMENT
IS THE CAUSE OF NEEDLESS SORROW
                AND PAIN · · · · · · ·

AS COMPARED TO
GOING WITH THE "FLOW"
OF THE MOMENT.

I DON'T KNOW WHERE TO BEGIN !

START FROM WHERE YOU ARE,

HERE, NOW !

Self

FEELING GOOD ABOUT MYSELF
ENHANCES THE WAY I SEE —
THE REST OF THE WORLD.

ALL OF OUR LIVES,
RUNNING · · · · · · · · ·
AWAY FROM OURSELVES · · · ·
AFRAID TO BE · · · ·
OURSELVES.

WHEN THERE IS NO
FEAR OF
THERE IS NO NEED TO DEFEND AGAINST

IT BEGINS WITH DO'S AND DON'TS,
SHOULD'S AND SHOULDN'TS,
"ACCEPTANCE" FOR BEING "GOOD",
"REJECTION" FOR BEING "BAD",
PROGRAMMED TO · · · · · FIT THE MOLD.

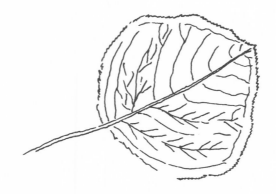

EXPERIENCING REJECTION IS THE
WORST OF HURTS.
WE WILL PAY ANY PRICE TO AVOID IT.

LOOKING BACK,
REFLECTING
WITHIN THE PERSPECTIVE OF TIME-DISTANCE.....
HOW TRAGIC THAT WE WASTE OUR LIVES
REACTING
INSTEAD OF REALIZING.

HOW IRONIC THAT THOSE WHOM WE LOVE
                              THE MOST
OFTEN BECOME THE SCAPEGOATS······
RECIPIENTS OF OUR INADEQUACIES.

          SHARED LOVE:
        THE ADHESIVE THAT
      HOLDS US-----TOGETHER.

HOW CAN I "JUST BE MYSELF"
WHEN I AM NOT CERTAIN OF
WHO I REALLY AM.

°

TO TRULY KNOW OURSELVES,
TO EXPERIENCE A SENSE OF SELF,
IS TO LIBERATE SELF OF THE NEED
FOR EXTERNAL "ANSWERS".

°

HAVING THE COURAGE TO BE OPEN,
RECEPTIVE....TO SOLICIT NEW IDEAS,
POINTS OF VIEW, RELEASES OUR
CREATIVE POWERS.

LET GO.......
FREE SELF OF EXCESS BAGGAGE.

°

TO EXPERIENCE
A SENSE OF SELF
WE MUST SLOW DOWN,
GET OFF THE MERRY-GO-ROUND,
DETACH SELF FROM
THE WORLD OF THINGS:
OBSERVE OUR TRUE NATURE,
EXPERIENCE THE ESSENCE OF
OUR BEING.

I AM FREE TO BECOME MYSELF
TO THE EXTENT THAT I AM ABLE . . . . .
TO DIRECT AND MONITOR MY THOUGHTS.

°

THE QUALITY OF OUR LIVES
IS IN PROPORTION TO
THE QUALITY OF OUR
ATTENTION.

°

THE "OLD TAPES",
THE PROGRAMMING, CONDITIONED MIND,
LIMIT OUR AWARENESS
OF THE MIRACLES UNFOLDING
BEFORE US . . . . . .
MOMENT TO MOMENT:
WATCH WHAT YOU ARE THINKING.

°

TO BE ALLOWED
THE FREEDOM TO MAKE
MISTAKES, THE INTEGRITY TO
ACCEPT THE CONSEQUENCES.
THE MATURITY TO EXTEND
THIS LATITUDE TO OTHERS.

I WAS WRONG!
WHAT'S WRONG WITH THAT?

WE NEED SOMEONE TO TALK TO
SOMEONE WHO WILL LISTEN.

A GOOD LISTENER HELPS US TO
"SEE THROUGH" THE PROBLEM
BY WITHHOLDING JUDGMENTS.

FEELING GOOD ABOUT MYSELF
ENHANCES THE WAY I SEE —
THE REST OF THE WORLD.

TOUCH ME, PLEASE······
BUT DON'T GET TOO CLOSE.

WE ACKNOWLEDGE OUR UNIQUENESS
AS HUMAN BEINGS
THEN PROCEED TO FIT EACH OTHER
INTO A COMMON MOLD.

LIKING - DISLIKING :
EGO REACTING TO A PRECONCEIVED
IMAGE.... AS A FACTOR OF ITS
CONGRUENCE WITH THE STORED,
BIOCOMPUTER, IMAGE.
(THAT'S A FUNNY LOOKING · · · · · · ·)

WHEN WE STOP LIKING AND DISLIKING
WE EXPERIENCE A NEW FREEDOM···
A NEW REALITY.

FREEING MYSELF FROM OLD BIASES AND
PREJUDICES ALLOWS ME TO DISCOVER
NEW TRUTHS
ON MY OWN.

UNIQUE AMONG ALL CREATURES,
WE HAVE THE CAPACITY FOR,
THE NEED TO CONNECT OURSELVES
TO, A SENSE OF PURPOSE OR MEANING
IN RELATION TO OURSELVES
AND THE UNIVERSE.

ALL OF US IN ONE WAY OR ANOTHER
ARE TRYING TO FIND OUT WHO WE ARE...
TO FEEL, TO EXPERIENCE, TO BE ABLE
TO DEFINE, ARTICULATE, A SENSE OF
PURPOSE IN OUR LIVES.

BLINDLY ACCEPTING TRADITION
CAN BE AN ILLUSION.
WE MUST SEARCH AND DISCOVER.......
FOR OURSELVES.

OUR LIVES SHOULD BE LIVED
PURPOSEFULLY - INTENTIONALLY
WITH SOMETHING GREAT IN MIND.

A SENSE OF SELF BECOMES AN AFFIRMATION
OF OUR WHOLENESS,
OUR CONNECTEDNESS WITH WHAT IS · · · ·
EXPERIENCING LIFE HOLISTICALLY,
SENSING THE INTERCONNECTIONS
OF MIND, BODY, AND SPIRIT,
LISTENING TO EACH,
INTEGRATING THEM INTO A
PEACEFUL WHOLE.

WE LONG FOR
STABLE VALUES AND RELATIONSHIPS
A MEANINGFUL, PURPOSEFUL
RELATIONSHIP TO LIFE
BUT ARE NOT WILLING
TO COMMIT OURSELVES
TO THE NECESSARY DISCIPLINES.

WE NEED TO EXPERIENCE
SOMETHING GREATER
THAN OURSELVES -----
TO FEEL FULFILLED
AS A HUMAN BEING.

DISCOVERING AND EXPERIENCING
OUR "CENTER"
THAT PLACE WHERE
WE FEEL AT PEACE
WITH OURSELVES
HELPS US TO "CONNECT".

WE MAY HAVE TO LET GO . . . . . OF
FREE SELF . . . . . FROM
EXTERNAL ATTACHMENTS
FOR IT TO MANIFEST (ITSELF)

EVERYTHING IN ITS TIME
AND PLACE .
DON'T PUSH "IT".

IF WE WERE NOT ATTACHED TO THINGS
WE WOULD HAVE NO-THING TO LOSE.

IT IS IN THE NATURE OF BEING HUMAN
TO WONDER
WHERE WE CAME FROM,
WHAT WE ARE · · · · · ·
IF THERE IS A PURPOSE TO
· · · · · · · OUR BEING.

EACH OF US IS UNIQUE
NO TWO EXACTLY ALIKE.
NEVER WAS, NEVER WILL BE.

LIFE SHOULD BE TAKEN SERIOUSLY-
BUT NOT TOO.

A SENSE OF HUMOR IS A PART OF WHAT
DISTINGUISHES HUMANKIND.

TO FULLY UNDERSTAND REALITY
AS A PROJECTION OF THE OBSERVER····
SEEING ONLY WHAT WE WANT TO SEE,
IS TO HAVE MADE A MAJOR BREAKTHROUGH
IN EXPERIENCING LIFE.

HAVING A FIXED IMAGE OF REALITY,
WE ARE OBLIGED TO DEFEND,
TAKE ISSUE WITH, QUALIFY,
REJECT:
ANYTHING THAT DOESN'T FIT·····

WE ARE PERCEIVED BY OTHERS
BY THE ROLES WE PLAY.

CHANGING THE ROLE
CHANGES THE IMAGE.

GROWTH, MATURITY, IMPLIES RISK-TAKING:
CHOICES
DECISIONS
COMMITMENT.

DEALING WITH LIFE IN TERMS OF
ABSOLUTES . . . . .
IS MORE COMFORTABLE . . . . .
LESS RESPONSIBLE.
NO NEED TO ADAPT-CHANGE,
NO UNCERTAINTIES,
NO NEED TO QUESTION,
NO NEED TO THINK.

WE LIVE IN A TIME,
ARE WITNESS TO,
WHAT MAY BE THE GREATEST
BREAKTHROUGH
OF HUMAN INSIGHT:
THE CONVERGENCE
OF SCIENTIFIC AND SPIRITUAL TRUTHS.

IT'S UP TO US . . . . .
TO DO . . . .
SOMETHING.

WE OFTEN REJECT
WHAT WE DON'T UNDERSTAND.....

AT OUR OWN EXPENSE.

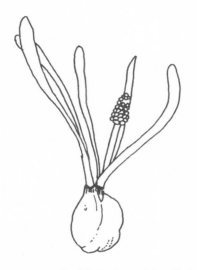

LET YOUR CONSCIENCE BE
YOUR GUIDE —
NOT REALLY -
CONSCIENCE IS TYPICALLY
GUILT RIDDEN.
BETTER TO TRUST INTUITION!
(IT HAS GOOD BLOOD LINES)

AN AUTHENTIC, PERSONAL COMMITMENT
TO A MODIFICATION OF ATTITUDE
AND BEHAVIOR CONGRUENT WITH
SELF IMAGE :

WHERE IT ALL BEGINS AND ENDS.
(TOO HEAVY ? THINK ABOUT IT.)

THE MILIEU, OUR CONTRIVED REALITY,
BLOTS OUT, OBSCURES, WHAT COULD BE.

IT'S NOT SO MUCH A MATTER OF
WITHDRAWING FROM THE MILIEU
AS IT IS SEEING THROUGH THE MILIEU
.......LESSENING ITS IMPACT........
LIVING WITH THE REALITIES.

WE SELDOM REACH A POINT IN OUR LIVES
WHERE WE WOULD NOT ENJOY THE EXPERIENCE
OF BEING PLEASANTLY SURPRISED:
A GIFT, PRAISE, RECOGNITION · · · · · · · · ·
A SURPRISE PARTY.

TEARS OF JOY.

WHERE AM I ALLOWING MY ENERGY
(PHYSICAL, MENTAL, SPIRITUAL)
TO TAKE ME ?

THE REALIZATION OF OUR POTENTIAL
COMES FROM THE INTEGRATION OF
BODY, MIND AND SPIRIT
EACH COMPLIMENTING, NOURISHING
THE OTHER

IMAGINATION
CREATIVITY
COURAGE :
MORE IMPORTANT THAN KNOWLEDGE.

WE DON'T BECOME FULLY AWARE OF OUR
ADDICTIONS, ATTACHMENTS, UNTIL WE
TRY TO CHANGE THEM:
FOOD, DRINK, HABITS, ATTACHMENTS,
ROUTINES, SECURITY. . . . .

OUR MOST PROFOUND EXPERIENCES,
TRUTHS, INSIGHTS, DO NOT LEND
THEMSELVES TO WORDS :
ARE INEFFABLE.
HOW THEN DO WE PASS THEM ON ?
DEEDS....... ACTIONS.....: BEHAVIOR.

THE GREAT TRUTHS
ARE THE SIMPLE TRUTHS.

RIGHT UNDER OUR NOSES.

WHAT IS THIS ELUSIVE INSIGHT WE SO
DESPERATELY PURSUE ?

WHY IS IT SO DIFFICULT TO ATTAIN ?

WHEN WE ARE "OUT OF OUR ELEMENT,"
A VARIETY OF COMPENSATORY, COPING,
ESCAPE MECHANISMS ARE ACTIVATED.
WE PUT ON A MASK, ASSUME A ROLE.

°

FOR THE MOST PART, OUR BEHAVIORS
ARE A MASK, A FACADE, A ROLE
CONTRIVED BY THE SUBCONSCIOUS
MIND TO OBSCURE THE TRUE SELF
..........A PROTECTIVE SHIELD,
A CAMOUFLAGE.

°

I MUST HAVE THE COURAGE TO TAKE
AN HONEST LOOK AT WHERE I
HAVE BEEN,
WHERE I AM, AND
WHERE I AM GOING.

WITHOUT APOLOGY.

BASIC TO THE UNDERSTANDING
OF SELF IS A SENSE OF WHOLENESS
.... IN RELATION
TO THE UNIVERSE.

KEEPING MY OPTIONS OPEN,
NOT PAINTING MYSELF INTO A CORNER,
NOT ALLOWING SELF TO BE CAUGHT UP
IN POLARIZED THINKING :

ALLOWING MY SELF TO GROW.

WE ARE NURTURED BY:

OPPORTUNITIES TO GROW
SPACE - SOLITUDE
TOLERANCE - PATIENCE
SEEING THE LIGHTER SIDE
COMPASSION - LOVE
ENTHUSIASM - LOVE OF LIFE

THE SICKNESS OF DISSATISFACTION.....
WITH WHAT WE ARE DOING·········

NO MATTER WHAT WE ARE DOING:

SELF - PITY !

PROGRESS IN EXPERIENCING
HIGHER LEVELS OF AWARENESS
MINIMIZES THE NEED FOR
MATERIAL "THINGS".

ONCE WE HAVE DETERMINED
OUR GOAL - TARGET -
WE SHOULD "LOCK ON" TO IT
WITH A COMMITMENT THAT INCLUDES
ACKNOWLEDGING AND ACCEPTING
THE PRICE TO BE PAID.

MENTAL SET : A BARRIER TO
THE COMMUNICATION OF IDEAS,
FEELINGS, THOUGHTS ······ FROM
ONE PERSON OR GROUP TO ANOTHER.
SEEING AND HEARING WHAT
WE WANT TO SEE AND HEAR.
SCREENING OUT THE INCOMPATIBLES.

FOR THE FIRST TIME IN OUR LIFE
TO REALIZE WHAT IT MEANS
TO TAKE THE TIME
TO · · · · · · · · · · ·

WE ALONE HAVE THE POWER TO PRESS
THE SWITCH THAT WILL TURN US ON.

TOO OFTEN
WE BREAK OUR SPIRIT
BY SELF - IMPOSED BURDENS:
SELF-INTIMIDATION
GUILT
FEAR
WHAT WOULD "THEY" THINK/SAY
IF I . . . .

FEELINGS OF DOUBT,
FEAR, INSECURITY --
IMMOBILIZE OUR SENSE OF SELF.

HUMANKIND HAS ALWAYS BEEN
ON THE CUTTING EDGE OF
DISCOVERING NEW TRUTHS.

NEVER HAS THE OPPORTUNITY
FOR BREAKTHROUGH
BEEN SO GREAT AS NOW.

EACH OF US, IN OUR OWN WAY,
             TRYING TO MAKE SENSE
                  . . . . OF LIFE.

THE TRAGEDY: WE REPRESENT
THE HIGHEST FORM OF CREATION
AND OUR OWN AWE/IGNORANCE
OF THE FACT PREVENTS US
FROM UNDERSTANDING · · · · · MUCH LESS
KNOWING.

THE WONDER OF THE UNIVERSE
THE MYSTERY WE SEEK TO UNRAVEL
IS NONE OTHER THAN
OURSELVES.

PERSONAL GROWTH
AWARENESS OF TRUE SELF
REQUIRES TIME, PATIENCE,
MOST OF ALL,
COMMITMENT.

WHEN WAS THE LAST TIME YOU SAT DOWN
AND HAD A GOOD TALK WITH YOURSELF?

REMINDING YOURSELF OF YOUR
POSITIVE, ALTRUISTIC ATTRIBUTES?

WE MUST TAKE TIME TO SORT OUT
OUR LIFE, DISCOVER OUR TRUE SELF.

THINK OF WHAT THE REAL YOU
COULD DO FOR THE REST OF US.

WE CAN SPEND OUR LIVES
LOOKING FOR . . . .
SOMEONE ELSE'S DEFINITION OF. . . . . . .
WHO WE ARE AND WHAT LIFE IS ALL ABOUT,
OR, WE CAN TRY TO UNDERSTAND . . . . . .
OURSELVES.

PREOCCUPATION WITH THE LITTLE THINGS,
TRIVIA, PREVENTS US FROM EXPERIENCING
THE WHOLENESS OF LIFE.

BROODING, GOSSIPING, NIT-PICKING,
BEING LAZY, NOT SUSTAINING
ATTENTION............
WE STRESS OURSELVES
BY ALLOWING OURSELVES
TO BECOME ANGRY, HOSTILE,
VIOLENT, FEARFUL,
UNCERTAIN, DEPRESSED.

THE TEST OF OUR CHARACTER,
INTEGRITY, MATURITY,
IS HOW WELL WE STAND UP UNDER
DURESS, EMOTIONAL STRESS.

IT'S NO GREAT CHALLENGE
TO BE GOOD WHEN
THINGS ARE GOING WELL.

HOW ARE YOU DOING?

WE CAN SPEND OUR LIVES
TRYING TO FIND OUT
WHAT LIFE IS ALL ABOUT.......
AT THE EXPENSE OF FINDING OUT
WHO WE ARE.

DON'T ALLOW SELF TO BE DRAWN INTO,
INTIMIDATED BY, A "GAME"
NOT OF YOUR CHOOSING.

THE "WE/THEY" PEOPLE NEED
ADVERSARIES: FODDER.
RESIST - REJECT.

SELF - PITY,
A NO-WIN GAME
...............OF
DIGGING OUR OWN
GRAVE.

LACKING A SENSE OF SELF
WE LIMIT OUR PERCEPTION OF REALITY.

SUCCESSFUL PEOPLE
HAVE A STRONG CONVICTION ABOUT,
BELIEF IN, THEMSELVES.

YOU WILL NEVER KNOW
IF YOU DON'T TRY—
DARE
TO BE
YOU.

OUR AUTHENTICITY (AS A PERSON)
IS ENHANCED TO THE DEGREE
THAT WE FREE
OURSELVES FROM EGO.

THE FALSE, ILLUSORY SENSE
CONJURED UP
BY OUR CONDITIONED STATE
OF MIND
PREVENTS US FROM REALIZING
OUR TRUE SELF....
OBSCURES THE SEARCH FOR
MEANING.

RESPONSIBILITY FOR SELF:
AN OUTGROWTH OF
A SENSE OF SELF.

OUR MATURITY AS HUMAN BEINGS,
A CULTURE, A CIVILIZATION,
IS A FACTOR, MAY BE JUDGED BY,
THE EXTENT TO WHICH WE ARE ABLE
TO FREELY ACCEPT AND CARRY OUT
RESPONSIBLE ACTS.

NO ONE ELSE CAN LIVE
OUR LIVES FOR US.
IT IS A UNIQUE, UNSHARED
RESPONSIBILITY.

EACH OF US MUST DECIDE, DETERMINE,
WHAT IS BEST FOR OURSELVES - IF OUR
LIVES ARE TO HAVE MEANING.

SENSORY ADDICTIONS, EGO NEEDS,
CANNIBALIZE THE BODY,
LEAVING LITTLE FOR INTELLECT
IN THE LATER YEARS.

MIND CANNOT BE AT PEACE
WHILE TORMENTED/
INTIMIDATED BY EGO.

WHEN THERE IS NO CONFLICT WITHIN,
THERE IS NO CONFLICT WITHOUT.

BEFORE WE KICK THE EGO,
WE SHOULD BE REASONABLY CERTAIN
THE PATIENT CAN WALK
WITHOUT A SUPPORT.

IF SELF THREATENS EGO,
EGO FIGHTS BACK..... WITH ESCAPE
MECHANISMS :
   COMPULSIVE EATING
   AND DRINKING,
   FATIGUE,
   PSYCHOSOMATIC ILLNESSES.
IT (EGO) FIGHTS FOR ITS LIFE
    (SURVIVAL).

BEHIND THE FACADE......
THE PROTECTIVE SHIELD
OF EGO....,IS AN INDIVIDUAL
IN SEARCH OF MEANING.

PLEASE DON'T MISTAKE MY EGO
   FOR MY SELF.

ONE OF THE CRUELEST TRICKS
EVER PLAYED ON US WAS
WHEN THE CULTURE INTO
WHICH WE WERE BORN
CAUSED US TO BELIEVE
WE HAVE TO APOLOGIZE
FOR BEING····· OURSELVES.

WE CAN "SPEND" OUR LIVES
TRYING TO EXPLAIN IT·····
TO OURSELVES, APOLOGIZING
FOR IT TO OTHERS, OR WE CAN
LIVE IT.

WATCH OUT FOR THE SHOULD'S
AND SHOULDN'TS
THEY CAN KILL········YOU.

EACH OF US HAS OUR OWN
PHYSICAL/ PSYCHOLOGICAL/
SPIRITUAL TERRITORY.

DON'T TRESPASS !

WE PROJECT SUBTLE SIGNS OF WARNING.

IF THERE IS NO COURAGE····
THERE ARE NO CONVICTIONS.

HAVE THE COURAGE,
FAITH IN SELF
TO LOOK AROUND THE CORNER,
TAKE THAT EXTRA STEP.

EVEN THOUGH WE HAVE
THOROUGHLY CONVINCED
OURSELVES OF THE
SOUNDNESS OF OUR POINT
OF VIEW · · · · · ·

IF IT DIFFERS DRAMATICALLY
FROM THE EXISTING MORES · · · ·
(CULTURE, CODE OF BEHAVIOR)
WE ARE IN TROUBLE.
(HERETIC, LUNATIC, ECCENTRIC,
                    RADICAL)

CREDIBILITY LIES SOMEWHERE
BETWEEN THE EXTREMES.
IF WE GET "TOO FAR OUT"
WE BECOME SUSPECT.

"VERY LITTLE IS NEEDED TO
    MAKE A HAPPY LIFE.
        IT IS ALL WITHIN YOURSELF,
        IN YOUR WAY OF THINKING."

                MARCUS AURELIUS

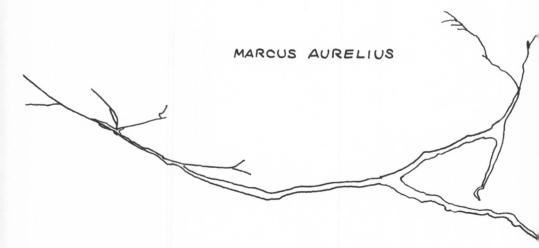

OUR PREOCCUPATION WITH OUR
ILLUSIONS OF KNOWLEDGE AND POWER
OBSCURES OUR NEED TO LOOK
WITHIN, TO BECOME AWARE OF OUR
TRUE NATURE, OUR INNER SELF.

THE FORCE WITHIN, THE ESSENCE,
TRUE SELF, MAY ONLY BE
DISCOVERED AND RELEASED
BY ELEVATING OUR LEVEL
OF CONSCIOUSNESS·······
AWAKENING.

TO BECOME LESS DEPENDENT
UPON FINDING AN ANSWER
"OUT THERE" AND MORE
CONFIDENT IN OUR OWN
CAPACITY FOR PERCEIVING
AN ANSWER FROM OUR
OWN INNER RESOURCES.

NO ONE ELSE CAN DO IT
FOR US.
THEY CAN ONLY POINT
THE WAY,
COMPASSIONATELY.

Child

TEACH A CHILD
BY EXAMPLE

TO SEE IN A CHILD · · · · ·
ONLY THE GOOD. (GOD)

•

WHAT WE FEED THE MIND
OF A CHILD
IS CRUCIAL TO THE SURVIVAL
OF HUMANKIND

TEACH A CHILD BY EXAMPLE.

◦

WE MUST STRIVE FOR
THE MATURITY
THAT WILL ALLOW US
· · · · ·TO ALLOW OUR CHILDREN· · · · ·
THE FREEDOM TO MATURE.

THE MOST PRECIOUS GIFT WE CAN
GIVE TO OTHERS, ESPECIALLY
CHILDREN, IS LOVE, PATIENCE
AND UNDERSTANDING.
NO AMOUNT OF MATERIAL WEALTH
CAN BUY THESE.

○

RIDICULE, ESPECIALLY OF THE YOUNG,
LEAVES AN INDELIBLE IMPRINT....
TEACHES THEM (US) TO RETREAT OR ATTACK.

○

WE ARE ATTRACTED TO THOSE WHO
PROJECT AN AUTHENTIC CARING.
CHILDREN SEEM TO HAVE A SIXTH
SENSE FOR IT.

CHILDREN EXPERIENCE
A SENSE OF SELF,
A SENSE OF AWE,
THAT COMES FROM THE BEAUTY AND
GRANDEUR OF THEIR
NATURAL SURROUNDINGS.

°

WHEN A CHILD DISCOVERS AND
EXPERIENCES MEANING,
IT BECOMES A PART OF THEIR SELF.

HUGGING OUR GRANDCHILDREN........

THE RE-EMBRACING OF OUR
        OWN CHILDREN:

LINKING THE PROCESS OF CREATION.

o

AWAKENING THE YOUNG CHILD EARLY IN
LIFE TO HIS OR HER POTENTIAL
INNER-STRENGTH, RESOURCES,
FOR PEACE AND TRANQUILITY,
RATHER THAN GOADING THEM
TO SEEK THE SHALLOW PLEASURES
OF THE SENSES AND THE EGO,
NURTURES THEIR SENSE OF SELF.

o

TOO PREOCCUPIED WITH SELF
TO BECOME INVOLVED IN ACTIVITIES
AT THEIR LEVEL ......
WE BUY OUR CHILDREN ....
FOOD, TOYS, GAMES, PLACES .....
THEN WONDER
LATER
WHERE THEY GOT THEIR
FUNNY IDEAS.

THE MOST POWERFUL FORCE
IN SHAPING THE LIVES
OF OUR CHILDREN—
MORE INDELIBLE THAN GENETICS—
IS THE IMPACT
OF OUR DREAMS,
ASPIRATIONS AND DISAPPOINTMENTS
AS EVIDENCED BY OUR EXAMPLE.

Others

THOSE CLOSEST --- TO US
SOMETIMES KNOW US
THE LEAST.

LIFE HAS MEANING ONLY INSOFAR AS
IT IS SHARED . . . . WITH OTHERS.

°

WE NEED THE PRESENCE OF OTHERS
. . . . LOVING THEM . . . . . . AS THEY ARE.

°

IF WE CAN'T RELATE TO ANOTHER
HUMAN BEING LOVINGLY . . . .
WE SHOULD EXAMINE OUR MOTIVES.

°

OUR CREDIBILITY EVOLVES FROM THE
CONSISTENCY AND CONGRUENCE
BETWEEN OUR PROJECTED SELF
AND OUR BEHAVIOR . . . . DEEDS.

THERE IS ONLY ONE SIN:

TO ABUSE, DEMEAN, INJURE, EXPLOIT,
ANOTHER HUMAN BEING . . . . .
BY THOUGHT, WORD OR DEED.

CONTINUALLY HURTING ONE ANOTHER
WITHOUT MALICE AFORETHOUGHT.....
THE TRAGEDY.......
THAT WE DO IT UNCONSCIOUSLY
......WITHOUT THINKING......OF
CONSEQUENCES.
INSENSITIVE TO THE HUMAN PREDICAMENT.

o

OUR PERCEPTIONS AND FEELINGS
CONCERNING ONE ANOTHER
ARE PROJECTIONS OF EXPECTATIONS····

MIRRORED BACK.

o

NOT ONLY DO WE SEE WHAT
WE WANT TO SEE,
"OTHER" ONLY SHOWS WHAT HE OR SHE
WANTS TO REVEAL.

o

THE QUALITY OF OUR RELATIONSHIP
TO OTHERS DETERMINES THE EXTENT
TO WHICH WE WILL EXPERIENCE
OUR HUMAN-NESS.

DON'T ALLOW YOURSELF
TO BE TO BE INTIMIDATED
BY THE EXPECTATIONS OF OTHERS.
THEY DON'T SEE · · · · · ·
WHAT YOU SEE !

o

TO JUDGE ANOTHER ON THE BASIS
OF INHERITED CHARACTERISTICS,
TRAITS OVER WHICH ONE HAS NO CONTROL,
IS TO NURTURE EGO-CENTRICITY
AND CONDEMN ONESELF TO A
WORLD OF ILLUSION.

o

I WILL ACCEPT OTHERS WITHOUT
JUDGEMENT; WITHOUT CRITICISM.

THERE BUT FOR THE GRACE OF GOD
GO I .

o

TO INSPIRE EACH PERSON WE TOUCH
IN A WAY THAT WILL CAUSE THEM
TO FEEL BETTER ABOUT THEMSELVES:
ENHANCE THEIR SELF-ESTEEM,
LISTENING, COMPLIMENTING,
ENCOURAGING, CARING · · · · · · ABOUT

TO IMPOSE OURSELVES
ON OTHERS IS TO NEUTRALIZE
A PORTION OF THEIR POTENTIAL
FOR REALIZING THEMSELVES.

o

IF I ALLOW
SOME OF THINGS YOU DO
TO ANNOY ME ......
THAT IS NOT FAIR
........, TO EITHER OF US.

o

MUCH OF WHAT WE CONSIDER
TO BE PERSONAL ACCOMPLISHMENT
IS THE RESULTS OF ASSISTS FROM OTHERS.
OPENING DOORS ......
POINTING THE WAY.

THOSE CLOSEST TO US . . . . .
SOMETIMES KNOW US THE LEAST.

BE CAREFUL ABOUT LETTING
   SOMEONE ELSE
      TELL YOU WHAT'S GOOD
      FOR YOU.

            o

   WE KNOW WHAT'S GOOD
      FOR OURSELVES . . . . .
         IF WE WILL BE HONEST

         WITH OURSELVES.

            o

      THE AUDACITY OF
         ONE HUMAN BEING
            ASSUMING THE RIGHT
               TO POSSESS ANOTHER · · · ·

            AT ANY AGE.

IT'S THE INTERPLAY, THE GIVE AND TAKE,
WITHIN THE MILIEU, THAT ENABLES US
TO SURVIVE.

I MUST RESPECT THE DIGNITY,
THE TERRITORY,
OF ANOTHER'S MIND,
BEING CAREFUL NOT TO INTRUDE
BY TOUCHING, VIOLATING CONVERSATION,
IF I AM TO CONTRIBUTE
TO THEIR GROWTH.

ACCEPT ME AS I AM,
THAT WE MAY DISCOVER
ONE ANOTHER.

OUR MOTIVATION FOR MAKING CONTACT
WITH ANOTHER PERSON
IS OFTEN OUR NEED
TO BE LISTENED TO,
RECOGNIZED,
PRAISED.

OUR LIVES WILL BE ENHANCED
IN PROPORTION TO
THE GENUINE INTEREST WE SHOW
FOR THE INTERESTS OF OTHERS.

TO THE DEGREE THAT WE REACT
TO PETTINESS IN OTHERS......
WE BECOME A PART OF THE PETTINESS.

o

WE OFTEN DON'T KNOW ONE ANOTHER.
WE RESTRICT OUR VISIBILITY (TO OTHERS)
AND, AT THE SAME TIME,
ARE TRANSPARENT IN THE GAMES
WE PLAY.

o

WE DON'T TRUST ONE ANOTHER.

o

RARELY, IF EVER, DO WE ENGAGE
IN SERIOUS CONVERSATION,
FREE OF INTIMIDATION,
DEFENSIVENESS,
AGGRESSIVENESS,
EXPLOITATION.

A LOVING PERCEPTION OF OTHER
DOES TWO THINGS:
AVOIDS, OR AT LEAST MINIMIZES,
THE POSSIBILITY OF MIS-UNDERSTANDING.
RELIEVES MIND OF BURDENS OF GUILT,
FRUSTRATION, BIAS, TENSION, STRESS.

°

THE EVER SO SUBTLE MOVEMENT,
A BARELY PERCEIVED GLINT
IN ANOTHER'S EYE,
A NUANCE OF VOICE,
THAT COMMUNICATES THAT WE ARE
ON THE SAME "TRACK", THE SAME
WAVE LENGTH.

SENSING "CONNECTIONS" BETWEEN
HUMAN BEINGS THAT ARE MUCH
MORE PROFOUND AND SUBTLE THAN
WE HAVE EVER IMAGINED.

WHAT MORE CAN WE DO
THAN CARE FOR, COMFORT,
ONE ANOTHER?

°

WE CANNOT LIVE WHOLE-LY (HOLY)
WITHOUT (CARING FOR)
ONE ANOTHER.

°

THERE SHOULD BE PEOPLE
IN OUR LIVES WE BELIEVE IN
AND TRUST........UNCONDITIONALLY

NO MATTER WHAT HAPPENS.

TO WHAT EXTENT SHALL WE ALLOW
OURSELVES TO BE IMPACTED,
INTIMIDATED, BY THE INSECURITY,
GUILT, AND DEFENSIVE BEHAVIORS
OF OTHERS ?

IS AN UNCONDITIONAL COMPASSION,
PATIENCE, FORGIVENESS, POSSIBLE ?

        o

WHEN I "LISTEN" TO YOU
I HAVE TWO "PROGRAMS" IN MIND.
I TRY TO PROVIDE YOU AN OPPORTUNITY
TO GET SOME THINGS "OFF YOUR MIND"
AND TO POSE QUESTIONS THAT WILL ALLOW
YOU TO EXPLORE DIFFERENT "ANGLES"...
OF WHAT YOU SEEM TO BE CONCERNED
                    ABOUT.

        o

ASSUME THE BEST IN OTHERS
AND ACT TOWARD THEM ACCORDINGLY.

        o

IF WE CANNOT SAY SOMETHING NICE ......
WE SHOULDN'T SAY ANYTHING.
THERE IS ALWAYS SOMEONE OUT THERE
WHO NEEDS TO HEAR SOMETHING GOOD
FOR A CHANGE.
A COMPLIMENT, A WORD OF ENCOURAGEMENT,
PLEASE, THANK YOU.

AFRAID······

TO EXPOSE
TRUE SELF.

WHEN YOU TRUST ME, YOU ARE TRUSTING
YOURSELF..........
CONFIRMING YOUR FAITH IN SELF.

TO HAVE EARNED SOMEONE'S TRUST
IS A COMPLIMENT:
AN AWESOME RESPONSIBILITY.

o

IF YOU MUST ASK THE QUESTION,
"CAN I TRUST YOU?"............
YOU HAVE ANSWERED THE QUESTION.

o

TRUST INTUITION.
THERE ARE DIRECTIONS
WHICH COME FROM WITHIN -
DEFYING LOGIC AND REASON.
RADIATING YOUR OWN TRUTH-ESSENCE:
FOLLOW YOUR LEAD.

TWO MINDS MEETING:

INTUITIVE CONVERGENCE.

Peace of Mind

BEING AT PEACE
WITH OURSELVES
ENHANCES THE PROSPECT
OF OUR BEING AT PEACE
WITH OTHERS

PEACE OF MIND
COMES FROM LETTING GO,
FREEING SELF
OF THE ENCUMBRANCES
OF THE CONDITIONED MIND.

○

PEACE OF MIND
EVOLVES FROM A SENSE OF SELF,
WHICH EVOLVES FROM
ATTENDING TO WHAT IS :
(OF THE MOMENT)

A DYNAMIC UNFOLDING.

○

BEING AT ONE WITH :
MOVING ONE'S MIND, BODY, LANGUAGE
IN A "GRACEFUL" FLOW :
GENTLE, SENSITIVE, NOT HURRIED,
SOFT, DELICATE, PLEASING, CENTERED :
SIMPLE ELEGANCE.

○

A PASSIVE, RECEPTIVE FLOWING MOOD
INVITES PEACE OF MIND.

SHE HAD ENLIGHTENED EYES
PROJECTING PEACE OF MIND.
CLEAR, BRIGHT, UNINTIMIDATED,
SEEING. . . . . .THROUGH.

TO HAVE SEEN THROUGH IT ALL :
THE ULTIMATE UNDERSTANDING,
ENLIGHTENMENT · · · · · PEACE OF MIND.

RAPTURE ?
ECSTASY ?

o

THE PEACE OF MIND WE SEEK
IS NOT SO MUCH
"DOING SOMETHING ABOUT"
AS IT IS
"ALLOWING IT TO HAPPEN". . . . . .
ACCEPTING THE REALITY OF HERE
                    AND NOW.

o

THE GREATER THE CONGRUENCE
BETWEEN EXPECTATIONS AND OUTCOMES,
THE GREATER THE PEACE OF MIND.

o

PEACE OF MIND COMES FROM
A FEELING WITHIN OURSELVES,
A KNOWING, THAT WE CAN COUNT ON
OURSELVES, CAN BELIEVE
IN OURSELVES.

ONCE WE HAVE EXPERIENCED
PEACE OF MIND
IT FOLLOWS WHEREVER WE GO ······
"TOUCHING" ······ OTHERS.

IF WE ARE AT PEACE WITH OURSELVES
WE ENHANCE THE PROSPECT OF OUR
BEING AT PEACE WITH OTHERS.

Deeds

BEYOND THE RHETORIC —

WORDS
WITHOUT DEEDS
MAKE A MOCKERY OF BEING HUMAN.

o

OUR ACTIONS DISSOLVE THE RHETORIC
OF OUR VALUES.
OUR WORDS BECOME TRANSPARENT,
HOLLOW, EMPTY · · · ·
FOR LACK OF CONGRUENT BEHAVIOR.

o

HUMANKIND'S DILEMMA IS,
HAS ALWAYS BEEN,
THE CONTRADICTION THAT EXISTS
BETWEEN OUR WORDS AND OUR DEEDS.

WE, AS A SPECIES, HAVE BEEN
UNWILLING TO COMMIT OURSELVES
TO THE WORK · · · · · · THE NECESSARY
DISCIPLINE · · · · · OF SUSTAINED
ATTENTION - COMMITMENT TO OUR
BELIEFS,

OFTEN, IN RELATION TO NEWLY PERCEIVED
INSIGHTS, WE FEEL A COMPULSION
TO VERBALLY COMMUNICATE
THIS NEW-FOUND WISDOM, WHEN IN FACT,
IT MIGHT BETTER BE INTERNALIZED
WITHIN OURSELVES AND COMMUNICATED
BEHAVIORALLY.

o

BEYOND THE RHETORIC OF
AFFIRMATION :
COMMITMENT , DEEDS.

o

WE CREATE OUR (OWN) IMMORTALITY
BY THE IMPRESSIONS AND IMPRINTS
WE LEAVE ON THE MINDS OF THOSE
WHO WILL SURVIVE :
HOW WE HAVE BEHAVED.

o

THE QUALITY OF OUR LIVES
IS MEASURED BY DEEDS,
NOT POSITION OR POSSESSIONS.

WE CAN MAKE A DIFFERENCE
IN THE QUALITY OF LIFE
AVAILABLE TO HUMANKIND······
IF WE WILL REPLACE RHETORIC
WITH DEEDS.

Commitment
(THE WORK)

WHO SAID IT WOULD BE EASY?

THE REALIZATION OF OUR HUMAN
POTENTIAL REQUIRES A COMMITMENT
TO THE WORK:
FREEING OURSELVES FROM THE
CONDITIONED MIND, ADDICTIONS,
ATTACHMENTS.

SLOTH LAZINESS, INERTIA, CAN ONLY
BE OVERCOME BY THE APPLICATION
OF ONE-POINTED ATTENTION TO
WILL.

○

FREEING OURSELVES OF INGRAINED
HABITS, ADDICTIONS, CAN BE
THE MOST DIFFICULT WORK
WE CAN EXPERIENCE..... OR THE
EASIEST...DEPENDING UPON WHERE
OUR MIND IS······ COMING FROM.

○

THE PRICE OF PERSONAL FREEDOM
FREEDOM OF SELF.......
IS MORE THAN MOST OF US ARE
WILLING TO PAY.

○

I MAY NOT BE TOO CLEAR ON WHAT
NEEDS TO BE DONE, BUT I
CERTAINLY KNOW WHAT I SHOULD
<u>NOT</u> DO.

PRACTICE WHAT YOU KNOW······ IS RIGHT.

ONCE WE REALIZE WE ARE PLAYING
A TRAGIC, DEADLY GAME, WITH,
ON OURSELVES . . . .
WE CAN CHANGE THE GAME . . . .
BUT NOT WITHOUT GREAT EFFORT.

WE START BY DARING TO THINK
ABOUT THE CONTRADICTIONS,
THE ABSURDITIES, THE EFFECTS
OF CONDITIONING (PROGRAMMING)
AND THE INFINITE-NESS OF OUR
OPTIONS :
ALTERNATIVE BEHAVIORS.

THE "DOING" IS THE THING. IT REQUIRES
A MENTAL, ATTITUDINAL DISCIPLINE.
A REPROGRAMMING. A SUSTAINED
ATTENTION, MONITORING, TO STAY
ON COURSE.

MOTIVATION IS AN ILLUSIVE INTANGIBLE.

THE "WORK" BEGINS WITH PAYING ATTENTION
TO WHERE WE ARE AND WHAT ASPECT
OF OURSELVES IS BEING EXPOSED.
NOT RETREATING, DWELLING IN, OR
SEEKING SECURITY IN THE PAST NOR
FANTASIZING ABOUT OR FEARING AN
UNKNOWABLE FUTURE.
NOT COMPLAINING, LIKING, OR DISLIKING,
JUDGING OR ATTACHING TO......
ACUTELY AWARE OF THE BEAUTY
OF THE MOMENT.
SEEING GOD IN ALL THINGS.
COUNTING OUR BLESSINGS.
FREEING OURSELVES TO TRANSCEND,
BE REBORN:
TO TRANSFORM SELF.

MANY OF US HAVE A TENDENCY
TO FOLLOW THE LINE OF LEAST RESISTANCE:
TO COMPULSIVELY "LATCH ON" TO ANYTHING
THAT COMES ALONG · · · · · · ·
IF IT SUGGESTS THE POSSIBILITY
OF AN EASY WAY OUT.
IT WON'T HAPPEN THAT WAY:
THERE ARE NO EASY ANSWERS
"OUT THERE."

WE MUST MAKE A MORE SINCERE EFFORT
TO UNDERSTAND · · · · · · THAT WE MUST
LOOK WITHIN OURSELVES FOR THE ONLY
ANSWERS THAT CAN HAVE MEANING.

TOTAL COMMITMENT:
A RIGOROUS DISCIPLINE TO PURGE
THE MIND OF TRIVIA, TO NEUTRALIZE
THE OLD TAPES, REPROGRAM THE
BIO - COMPUTER.

SURE WE CAN - IF WE WILL BE HONEST
WITH OUR SELF.

UNCONDITIONAL BELIEF IN SELF:
TOTAL COMMITMENT.

IT SEPARATES THE ACTUALIZERS
FROM THE DREAMERS,
THE PROCRASTINATORS.

o

MOST OF US ARE UNWILLING
TO MAKE THE EFFORT,
TO ASCEND THE LADDER
LEADING OUT OF THE PIT.

WE WASTE OUR TIME
ADMIRING THE LADDER.

o

WHO SAID IT WOULD BE EASY?

IF
THE DISCIPLINE
BECOMES
BOTH MEANS AND END
IT'S TIME TO GO BACK
TO SQUARE ONE.

AFTER LISTENING TO ALL THE ADVICE,
READING ALL THE BOOKS.....
IF WE ARE AWAKE,
WE BEGIN TO SENSE THAT
"SOMETHING IS MISSING"........

THE WORDS, CONCEPTS, DOGMA, RITUAL,
ARE NOT ENOUGH.

THEY LEAVE US EMPTY, UNFULFILLED.

THE ELEMENT THAT IS GLOSSED OVER
OFTEN LEFT OUT
IS THE CRITICAL FACTOR OF WILL,
INVOLVING DISCIPLINE
AND A QUALITY OF ATTENTION
ALIEN
TO MOST READERS / SEEKERS.

THE WORK, THE COMMITMENT,
EVOLVES FROM A PROGRESSIVE
HIERARCHY OF INDIVIDUAL,
PERSONAL RESPONSIBILITIES:
AWAKENING TO THE "POSSIBILITIES"—
ONE-POINTED ATTENTION TO THE
DIRECTION OF OUR THOUGHTS -
REPROGRAMMING . . . . . .PRAYER MANTRA.

"AWAKENING" IS THE REALIZATION
THAT OUR BEHAVIOR IS LARGELY
THE RESULT OR PRODUCT OF A
CONDITIONED, PROGRAMMED MIND.

THEN . . . . . . THE WORK OF . . . . UN-DOING.

UNTIL WE COMMIT OURSELVES
TO THE WORK,
OUR MISSION IN LIFE
IS AN ILLUSION,
A FRAUD, A FANTASY . . . .
DOES NOT EXIST.

THERE ARE NO FREE RIDES
NO SHORT CUTS
THE PIPER MUST BE PAID,
KNOWLEDGE AND RHETORIC
LEAD NOWHERE . . . .
WITHOUT A COMMITMENT TO
THE NECESSARY DISCIPLINE
OF ATTENTION . . . .
TO WHERE WE ARE COMING
FROM - AT THE MOMENT - TO -
MOMENT.

Quiet Mind

WE HAVE A NEED FOR SPACE
AND SOLITUDE : TIME TO BE ALONE-
TO THINK, TO DREAM, TO WONDER.

WE WILL NOT EXPERIENCE
MOMENTS OF INSIGHT
UNTIL WE CLEAR THE CHANNELS,
STOP THE INCESSANT CHATTERING
OF THE MANY ASPECTS OF EGO.

THE CEASELESS, SENSELESS
CHATTERING OF THE MIND —
DRAINS OUR ENERGIES
(PARTICULARLY WHEN NEGATIVE
ATTITUDES AND EMOTIONS
ARE INVOLVED)

MIND, BY ITS NATURE, ALWAYS,
PROBING, SEEKING, COMPARING :
"PROGRAMMING" — RESISTS
SUSTAINED ATTENTION.

PREOCCUPATION WITH, ADDICTION TO
THOUGHTS — LIMITS OUR PERCEPTION
OF WHAT'S GOING ON ⋯⋯ AROUND US.

THE KEY CONCEPT, IN RELATION TO
QUIETING THE MIND IS — "LETTING GO"—
STOPPING THOUGHTS, FREEING ONES
SELF FROM STRESS AND TENSION.

FIND A QUIET PLACE —
TAKE A DEEP BREATH
(A SIGH OF RELIEF ?)
RELAX YOUR BODY
ONE - POINTEDLY, FOCUS, CONCENTRATE
ONE - A SINGLE THOUGHT OR SOUND.

TOO BUSY TO RELAX ?
IT'S NOT EASY: "BUSY" CAN
BE AN EXCUSE FOR AVOIDING
A COMMITMENT TO
THE DISCIPLINE.

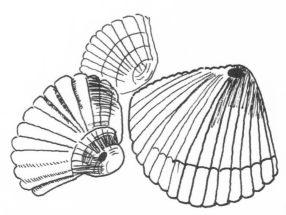

OUR ABILITY TO QUIET THE MIND
IS A REFLECTION OF
OUR ABILITY TO CONTROL SELF.

MINDFULNESS IS SO FOREIGN
TO OUR USUAL MIND-LESS-NESS
THAT WE EXPERIENCE GREAT
DIFFICULTY IN DISCIPLINING
OURSELVES TO SUSTAINED ATTENTION.

THE QUIET MIND, FOCUSED IN
THE HERE AND NOW —
NOT LIKING OR DISLIKING —
ALLOWS US TO EXPERIENCE
OUR TRUE, AUTHENTIC SELF.

QUIET TIME CAN PROVIDE
AN OPPORTUNITY – TO PUT
SOME DISTANCE, SPACE,
BETWEEN OURSELVES AND
OUR PROBLEM: OFFERS A
NEW PERSPECTIVE.

CONCERN FOR QUIETING THE MIND
SHOULD NOT BE A SOMETIME
EXERCISE – BUT RATHER AN
AROUND THE CLOCK AWARENESS
OF WHERE OUR THOUGHTS ARE:
AT ALL TIMES – IN ALL ACTIVITIES.

ALTHOUGH IT HELPS TO HAVE
ONES SPECIAL PLACE – FOR
QUIETING THE MIND – IT CAN
BE PRACTICED – EXPERIENCED
WHEREVER WE HAPPEN TO BE.

THE REGULAR PRACTICE OF
QUIETING THE MIND
DOES MORE TO RESTORE,
REVITALIZE ENERGY LEVELS
THAN DEEP SLEEP.

THE QUIET MIND CAN PROVIDE US
WITH THE RARE AND UNIQUE
EXPERIENCE OF SEEING THINGS
CLEARLY — AS THEY ARE —
FOR THE FIRST TIME IN OUR LIFE.

IN THE CLARITY OF A STILL AND OPEN
MIND TRUTH WILL BE REFLECTED

TO TRY TO CHANGE WHAT IS
ONLY SETS UP RESISTANCE

WITHOUT ANY THOUGHT FOR OURSELVES
SIMPLY BE.

LAO TSU

Epilogue

ONLY BY ASSUMING INDIVIDUAL
RESPONSIBILITY FOR SELF
WILL HUMANKIND REALIZE
ITS POTENTIAL, ITS DESTINY,
ITS DIVINITY.

°

WE MUST EMERGE FROM OUR COCOON.
THE TRANSFORMATION IS OVERDUE,
THE GESTATION PERIOD PAST.

°

THE SALVATION OF HUMANKIND
WILL COME FROM THE EMERGENCE
AND MANIFESTATION
OF CONSCIOUSNESS, WHICH WELLS UP
FROM A UNIVERSAL SENSE OF SELF.

°

THE SURVIVAL OF THE SPECIES
IS CONTINGENT UPON OUR ABILITY
TO CARE FOR ONE ANOTHER · · · · · · ·
INCLUDING THAT OTHER ASPECT
OF CREATION WE CALL NATURE.

THE TIME HAS COME . . . .
HAS ALWAYS BEEN,
FOR US TO ASSUME
PERSONAL RESPONSIBILITY
FOR BEING HUMAN :
TO COMMIT OURSELVES
TO HUMANKIND.

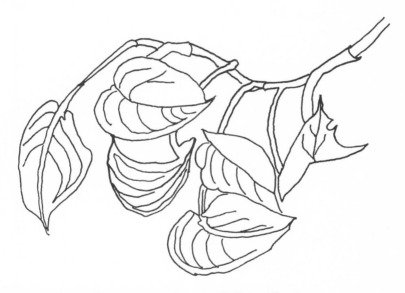

STANDING AT THE THRESHOLD,
WHICH OF OUR MANY OPTIONS
          WILL WE CHOOSE ?

          °

EACH OF US HAS THE INBORN POTENTIAL
FOR BECOMING A MODEL OF HUMANKIND.

THESE OBSERVATIONS ARE BUT TRUTHS....
OF WHICH WE NEED TO OCCASIONALLY
REMIND OURSELVES.

•

THIS BOOK DOES NOT HAVE THE ANSWERS-
RATHER IT POINTS A WAY
FOR YOU TO DISCOVER
THE ANSWERS.....
THAT LIE WITHIN YOURSELF.

•

THE SAME OLD PLATITUDES?
WHETHER THEY ARE OR NOT
DEPENDS
UPON US.......

ARE WE LOOKING FOR A WAY OUT
OR AN EXCUSE?

•

IF YOU ENJOYED THIS BOOK,
IF THE EXPERIENCE HAS
REMOVED SOME VEILS......
PASS IT ON TO A FRIEND.

A SENSE OF SELF
IS INCOMPLETE
WITHOUT A SENSE OF SPIRIT
(MY NEXT BOOK)

ADDITIONAL COPIES OF THIS BOOK
MAY BE ORDERED DIRECTLY FROM
THE PUBLISHER IF NOT AVAILABLE
AT YOUR LOCAL BOOK STORE OR
GIFT SHOP. TO ORDER BY MAIL,
SEND CHECK OR MONEY ORDER FOR $ 6.95
TO:

HELDON PRESS
9146 ARRINGTON AVE.
DOWNEY, CALIF. 90240

PLEASE INCLUDE $ 1.00 FOR POSTAGE
AND HANDLING. CALIFORNIA RESIDENTS
ADD 6 ½ % SALES TAX.